PERRON FAMILY HAUNTING

THE GHOST STORY THAT INSPIRED HORROR MOVIES

—◆◈❏ BY EBONY JOY WILKINS ❏◈◆—

CAPSTONE PRESS
a capstone imprint

Snap Books are published by Capstone Press
1710 Roe Crest Drive, North Mankato, Minnesota 56003
www.capstonepub.com

Library of Congress Cataloging-in-Publication Data
Names: Wilkins, Ebony, author.
Title: Perron family haunting : the ghost story that inspired horror movies /
by Ebony Joy Wilkins.
Description: North Mankato, Minnesota : Snap Books, an imprint of Capstone
Press, [2020] | Series: Snap. Real-life ghost stories. | Includes
bibliographical references and index. | Audience: Ages: 8-14.
Identifiers: LCCN 2018061102| ISBN 9781543573411 (hardcover) | ISBN
9781543574807 (pbk.) | ISBN 9781543573503 (ebook pdf)
Subjects: LCSH: Ghosts—Rhode Island—Juvenile literature. | Ghost
stories—Juvenile literature. | Perrin family—Juvenile literature. |
Haunted houses—Juvenile literature.
Classification: LCC BF1472.U6 W544 2020 | DDC 133.1—dc23
LC record available at https://lccn.loc.gov/2018061102

Editorial Credits
Eliza Leahy, editor; Brann Garvey, designer; Tracy Cummins, media researcher;
Tori Abraham, production specialist

Photo Credits
Alamy: AF archive, 5, Collection Christophel © 2013 Warner Bros Entertainment, 25, 27, 29, TCD/Prod.
DB, 7; Getty Images: Bettmann, 22, Russell McPhedran/Fairfax Media, 21; iStockphoto: sdominick, 19;
Newscom: Alberto E. Tamargo/Sipa USA, 26; Shutterstock: avtk, Design Element, Chantal de Bruijne,
Design Element, daniilphotos, 10, dzentry, 15, Fer Gregory, 9, Giraphics, Design Element, GoMixer, Design
Element, Joe Therasakdhi, 17, Lario Tus, Cover, MagicDogWorkshop, Design Element, NikhomTreeVector,
Design Element, NinaMalyna (frame), 9 Left, 25, Olivier Le Queinec, 13, Peter Horrox, 8, Prokrida (frame),
9 Top, 9 Right

Direct Quotations
Page 6: http://www.theoccultmuseum .com/the-conjuring-the-true-story-of-the-perron-family-haunting/
Pages 16–17: https://www.providencejournal.com/breaking-news/content/20130718-film-the-conjuring-
depicts-familys-reported-experience-with-paranormal-activity-in-burrillville-farmhouse-in-70s.ece
Pages 20–21: https://www.providencejournal.com/breaking-news/content/20130718-film-the-conjuring-
depicts-familys-reported-experience-with-paranormal-activity-in-burrillville-farmhouse-in-70s.ece
Page 26: https://www.ranker.com/list/true-story-behind-the-conjuring-movie/jacob-shelton
Page 26: http://www.trespassmag.com/qa-andrea-and-cynthia-perron-subjects-of-theconjuring/

Printed in the United States of America.
PA70

TABLE OF CONTENTS

HORROR IN HARRISVILLE

During the winter of 1970, Roger and Carolyn Perron wanted to find a home with more space for their five daughters, Andrea, Nancy, Christine, Cindy, and April. A farmhouse in rural Harrisville, Rhode Island, seemed to be the answer.

The 200-acre property was known as the Old Arnold Estate. The farmhouse had 14 rooms, a spacious porch, and plenty of room outdoors for the girls to play. But the family quickly realized that something wasn't right about their dream home. According to the family, they soon began to experience **paranormal** activity. Their story would eventually inspire the popular horror movie, *The Conjuring*.

To this day, people debate whether or not the hauntings at the Perron family home were real. Many people believe the family's accounts of paranormal activity. But **skeptics** believe that the family made up or exaggerated their stories in an attempt to make money and get attention from the media. Turn the page and decide for yourself. . . .

CHAPTER ONE

THE HAUNTING BEGINS

It didn't take long for the Perrons to determine they were not alone in their new home. When they moved in, the previous owner had a warning for them: "For the sake of your family, leave the lights on at night." But the Perrons didn't understand the warning at first. They unpacked their belongings, arranged the furniture, and explored their surroundings. As they did, strange noises, smells, and events **allegedly** began to occur.

MOVING TOYS

Cindy and the other Perron girls began to notice their toys were often left out of place. Cindy would set up whole villages of small toy figures. She would leave the room and soon come back to find the toys missing or rearranged. Sometimes the girls' toys would end up in the barn or in other areas around the Perrons' property. The sisters argued with one another about the missing and moved toys. But every time, the other girls would deny that they'd moved anything.

These strange events sometimes occurred when Cindy was alone in the house. She believed that someone besides her sisters must have moved her toys. Since she couldn't get rid of whoever was moving her toys, Cindy began to share them with the ghosts.

Carolyn Perron and her daughters on the steps of the family's Harrisville farmhouse

SURROUNDED BY SPIRITS

More unexplained **phenomena** soon began to occur. Doors allegedly slammed closed or proved impossible to open. Carolyn's broom went missing. It showed up in strange places without explanation. The Perron family often heard the sound of a broom sweeping. They found piles of dirt that appeared to have been swept up. But no one in the family claimed to have done the chore.

The family said that their clocks would stop at exactly 5:15 a.m. each morning. They said they often smelled something like rotten flesh wafting through their home.

OLD ARNOLD ESTATE

The Old Arnold Estate had been the home of eight different **generations** of the Arnold family. Some neighbors said that many of the residents had lived and died in the home, and their spirits had stayed behind. Carolyn would eventually research the history of the home and confirm that there had been many deaths on the property. The family believed this was the cause of the haunting they experienced.

SKEPTIC'S NOTE

The Old Arnold Estate was built in 1736. The noises heard in and around the house could be explained by the old structure of the home.

At night, the family heard strange noises. They claimed to hear voices coming from the walls. According to the family, they also spotted several ghosts. One was a little boy who wandered through the house. There was also a little girl who played with the daughters' toys. Sometimes they saw a woman wearing a gray dress, her neck bent at an odd angle, as though her neck was broken.

The events were strange, but not strange enough to trouble the Perrons too much. The spirits didn't seem angry. In fact, they seemed almost kind at times.

During the first two months of their stay at the house, Cindy reported that a ghost would tuck her into bed and kiss her goodnight. She said she knew it wasn't her mother, because the ghost smelled differently. But this loving behavior would soon change into something much more **sinister**.

FACT

During the 1970s, the United States economy experienced a **recession**. The Perron family said that money troubles were the main reason they could not leave their rural Rhode Island farmhouse.

CHAPTER TWO

LIVING WITH THE DEAD

According to the Perron family, the **atmosphere** of the home soon shifted. The ghosts seemed to be less kind and welcoming than before. The Perrons felt like they were constantly being watched.

Few people believed the Perrons, however. Even Roger had a hard time believing that there were spirits in the house. But the spirits were determined to make their **presence** known.

HIDE-AND-SEEK

It was a hot day in August, about six months after the family moved in. The girls decided to play their favorite game— hide-and-seek. The sprawling farmhouse and surrounding property were perfect for it. Cindy found a hiding spot in the woodshed. She climbed into a large wooden box and pulled the lid closed. She held a hand over her mouth to keep from giggling.

After waiting for a while, Cindy figured her sisters were not
going to find her. She tried to push at the top of the box
to get out. It didn't budge. The dark, tiny space began to
overwhelm Cindy. She started to panic. Cindy pushed harder
and began to pound at the lid. Later, she said it felt like
someone was sitting on top of it—like someone was holding
the lid closed. It was getting very hot inside. She began to feel
like she was running out of air.

Cindy screamed for help, but no one responded. Finally, after twenty minutes, Nancy found her and pulled open the box. According to the girls, they found no latches or locks on the box. The girls never discovered what it was that kept Cindy from escaping. They believed this was just one example of paranormal activity occurring in their new home.

EVIL SPIRITS

The paranormal activity began to get fiercer. Furniture allegedly **levitated** off the ground. The family said it sometimes slid straight across rooms. The girls' beds shook violently as they slept.

According to the daughters, one spirit pulled at the girls' limbs and hair while they slept. Another spirit allegedly lifted their beds and moved them around the bedroom. Yet another ghost is said to have hid in the corner of the girls' rooms. He stared at them with a terrifying grin as they played and slept.

Levitating furniture is often said to be a sign of the presence of spirits. However, skeptics believe that this phenomenon could be explained by people hallucinating, or imagining things that aren't there. The Perrons only have their own claims to back up these experiences. There is no proof that their furniture levitated.

Cindy claimed that one of the ghosts whispered into her ears at night. The spirit told her that seven dead soldiers were hidden in the walls of the house. She began to have awful nightmares.

Whenever the girls would yell for help, their parents couldn't hear them. According to Andrea, the house would somehow **muffle** their screams and cries.

As the spirits became physically **aggressive**, Roger and Carolyn knew they needed help. The family started to become scared for their safety. They now understood the previous owner's warning, ". . . leave the lights on at night." But even a well-lit home didn't seem to stop their difficult guests.

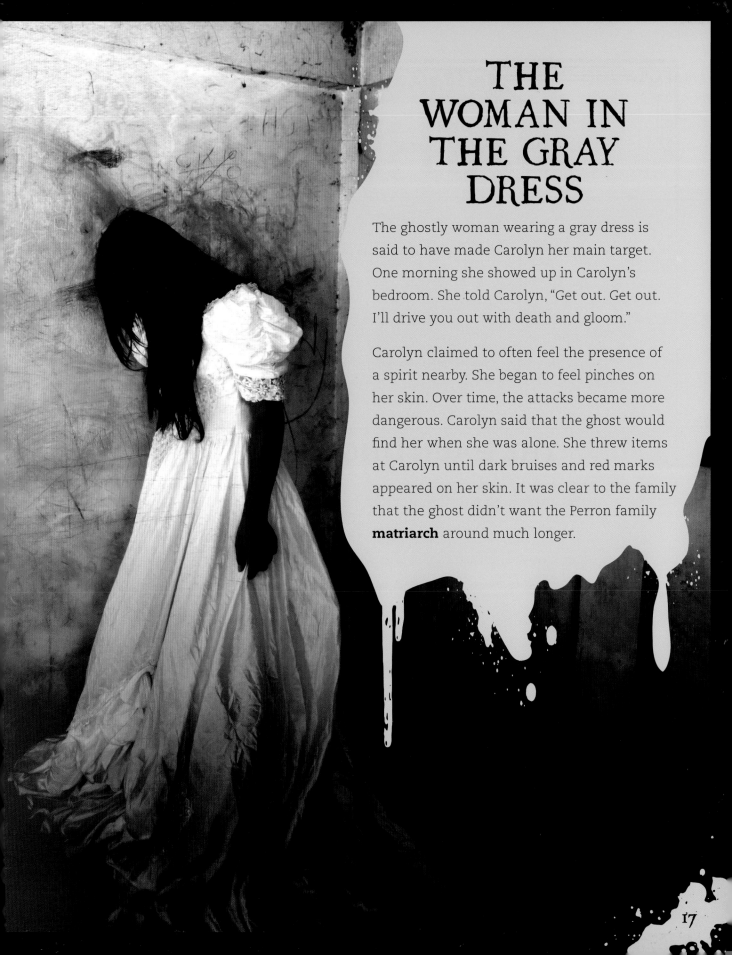

THE WOMAN IN THE GRAY DRESS

The ghostly woman wearing a gray dress is said to have made Carolyn her main target. One morning she showed up in Carolyn's bedroom. She told Carolyn, "Get out. Get out. I'll drive you out with death and gloom."

Carolyn claimed to often feel the presence of a spirit nearby. She began to feel pinches on her skin. Over time, the attacks became more dangerous. Carolyn said that the ghost would find her when she was alone. She threw items at Carolyn until dark bruises and red marks appeared on her skin. It was clear to the family that the ghost didn't want the Perron family **matriarch** around much longer.

CHAPTER THREE

BATHSHEBA

The Perron family believes that the ghost in the gray dress became angry when it was clear that they weren't going to flee the home. The ghost's actions were harsher and happened more and more frequently. She continued to haunt her favorite target in the Perron family—Carolyn.

THE HAUNTINGS WORSEN

The ghost apparently found Carolyn resting on the couch one evening. Carolyn felt a pain in her leg. She could also feel blood. She moved the blanket from her lap. The blood was coming from a single **puncture** wound on the side of her leg. Sometime during her nap, Carolyn believed she had been stabbed with something. The wound appeared to be the exact shape and size of a knitting needle. The family believed this was a sign that the ghost wanted Carolyn gone.

FACT

The oldest daughter, Andrea Perron, has written three books about her family's experiences living with spirits. The books are titled *House of Darkness House of Light*, volumes 1–3.

HELP ARRIVES

Word traveled about the reported hauntings at the Perron home. Lorraine and Ed Warren, a husband-and-wife team who were paranormal investigators, heard about the hauntings at the Old Arnold Estate. Lorraine and Ed Warren had founded the New England Society for **Psychic** Research. Ed studied **demons**, while Lorraine claimed to be able to communicate with demons and other evil spirits. The Warrens went to the Perron home to help the young family figure out what was going on.

Carolyn was relieved to have help. Many hadn't believed her claims of haunting, but the Warrens did. According to Andrea, when Lorraine walked into the Perron house she immediately told them, "I feel a dark presence, and her name is Bathsheba."

The Warrens agreed with Carolyn that the house was haunted by evil spirits. They believed Bathsheba was a witch. Legend says she murdered her child and then took her own life. The Warrens also believed there had been many other terrible events that had occurred on the Perron property, including unexplained accidents and deaths.

Over the course of their careers, Lorraine and Ed Warren claimed they took on more than 10,000 paranormal investigations.

SKEPTIC'S NOTE

Many don't agree with the legend of Bathsheba. Historical records show that a woman by the name of Bathsheba Thayer Sherman lived on the property in the 1800s. While she was originally charged in an infant's death, the charges were eventually dropped. Skeptics point to historical records that suggest Bathsheba was a respectable wife and mother. She cared for her children and the children of her neighbors. They believe the baby in her care could have simply died of natural causes or an accident.

Desperate to help the young family, the Warrens attempted to cleanse the home. They organized a **séance** to try to communicate with Bathsheba. Cindy and Andrea hid nearby to watch. The girls claimed to see their mother speak in a language they had never heard. They also said that Bathsheba lifted their mother in a chair and flung Carolyn's body across the room. The girls were terrified. They believed their mother had been **possessed** by Bathsheba.

In this image from 1986, Richard Busch from the Committee for Scientific Investigation of Claims of the Paranormal confronts Ed and Lorraine Warren.

FACT

The Warrens were **criticized** by many over the course of their careers. In 1997, the New England Skeptical Society (NESS) investigated the husband-and-wife team. They gave an interview on their findings in the *Connecticut Post*. NESS claimed that the Warrens produced little, if any, scientific proof of the hauntings they investigated.

THE AMITYVILLE HAUNTING

The Warrens were also famous for investigating the Amityville Haunting. This haunting was the basis for the book *The Amityville Horror*, by Jay Anson. Several films were also made based on the events in Amityville. Today people remain divided over whether or not the haunting was a **hoax**.

The haunting began in 1975. George and Kathy Lutz moved into a home at 112 Ocean Avenue on Long Island in New York. The home had been the scene of several murders just over a year before. Soon after the Lutz family arrived, the family claimed to notice strange sounds and smells, and experienced frightening events. They left the home less than a month after moving in.

CHAPTER FOUR

NIGHTMARE OVER?

Ultimately, the Perrons believed that the Warrens' attempts to help only made matters worse. Carolyn became weak and tired. She seemed to age quickly and was not acting like herself. The séance had been so out of control that Roger asked the Warrens to leave the home.

But even after the Warrens left, the Perrons claimed that the spirits remained. The family stayed in touch with the Warrens over the years, but they never were able to rid the family of Bathsheba's curse. The Perrons simply tried their best not to disturb Bathsheba and the other spirits until they could afford to leave Harrisville.

FACT

Roger Perron was often gone while the Perrons lived at the Old Arnold Estate. He often traveled away from home for work. He was rarely the target of any of the spirits in the house. He remained skeptical for a long time about what Carolyn and their daughters experienced.

Roger and Carolyn Perron
at the family home

The five Perron daughters in
front of the Harrisville home

AFTER THE MOVE

After ten years of living with evil spirits, the Perron family had had enough. In June 1980, they sold the property and moved to Georgia.

The farmhouse had other owners after the Perrons moved on. According to Andrea, many claimed to experience paranormal activity on the property. "The man who moved in to begin the restoration on the house when we sold it left screaming without his car, without his tools, without his clothing," Andrea said in an interview. "He never went back to the house . . . and it sat vacant for years."

Actress Joey King and Andrea Perron promote *The Conjuring* on a talk show.

With their move, the family hoped they were leaving the spirits behind. But Andrea later wrote about the spirits that apparently followed them to their new home. She claims that, to this day, the Perrons are haunted by Bathsheba's curse. "The house never left us, even though we left the house. It never left us and it never will," Andrea said.

THE CONJURING

The Conjuring is a horror movie inspired by the Perron family's experiences. The film was shot in North Carolina and directed by James Wan. Lorraine Warren gave the filmmakers advice on the project.

Similar to real life, the movie shows the Warrens helping the Perrons rid their home of the evil spirits. The Warrens bring in a team of paranormal investigators. Bathsheba is angered at their presence. She possesses Carolyn's body, just as the Perrons believe it occurred in real life. However, in the film, Bathsheba attempts to get Carolyn to hurt one of her children as she had done. There are no reports that Carolyn was tempted to hurt one of her daughters in real life.

The entire family was invited to the set during the filming of *The Conjuring*. Carolyn decided not to go at the last minute. While the daughters were giving an interview on the set, a wild wind is said to have torn through the area. Later the Perron daughters received bad news. They learned that Carolyn had fallen and broken her hip at the same time of this strange event. Andrea believes this was a sign from Bathsheba. The ghost was still haunting them—and warning them not to dig up the past.

Life with evil spirits was not what the Perrons had expected when they moved into their dream farmhouse. To this day, there is much debate over whether or not the haunting in Harrisville was a hoax. But whether these ghosts were real or imagined, the Perron family had to learn to live with them for the rest of their lives.

FACT

Vera Farmiga and Patrick Wilson played Lorraine and Ed Warren in *The Conjuring*. The actors spent several days learning from the real-life Lorraine Warren before they filmed. Farmiga and Wilson also starred in *The Conjuring 2*. The sequel is based on the Enfield Haunting in which a family in England was victim to a **poltergeist** haunting.

The real-life Perron sisters (top) pose on the set of *The Conjuring* with the actresses who played them in the movie (bottom).

SKEPTIC'S NOTE

Aside from their own claims, there is no proof that the Perron family experienced paranormal activity. A recent resident of the home, Norma Sutcliffe, believes they made it all up.

GLOSSARY

aggressive (uh-GRESS-iv)—tending toward or showing violent or threatening behavior

allegedly (uh-LEDGE-id-lee)—said to be true or to have happened, but without proof

atmosphere (AT-muhs-feer)—the mood or feeling that you get in a place or situation

criticize (KRIT-i-size)—to find fault with

demon (DEE-muhn)—a devil or an evil spirit

generation (jen-uh-RAY-shuhn)—a group of people born around the same time

hoax (HOHKS)—a trick that makes people believe something that is not true

levitate (LEV-i-tate)—to hover in the air

matriarch (MAY-tree-ark)—a woman who is the head of a family

muffle (MUHF-uhl)—to make a sound quieter or less clear

paranormal (pair-uh-NOR-muhl)—having to do with an event that has no scientific explanation

phenomenon (fe-NOM-uh-non)—a very unusual or remarkable event

poltergeist (POHL-tur-guyst)—a ghost that causes physical events, such as objects moving

possess (poh-ZESS)—to have complete power over someone

presence (PREZ-uhns)—a person or thing that exists in a place

psychic (SYE-kik)—relating to events that are not able to be explained by natural laws

puncture (PUHNGK-chur)—a hole made by a sharp object

recession (ri-SESH-uhn)—a time when business slows down and more workers than usual are unemployed

séance (SAY-ahnss)—a meeting in which one attempts to communicate with the spirits of the dead

sinister (SIN-uh-stir)—evil

skeptic (SKEP-tik)—someone who doubts or questions beliefs

READ MORE

Loh-Hagan, Virginia. *MacKenzie Poltergeist*. Urban Legends: Don't Read Alone! Ann Arbor, MI: Cherry Lake Publishing, 2018.

McCollum, Sean. *Handbook to Ghosts, Poltergeists, and Haunted Houses*. Paranormal Handbooks. North Mankato, MN: Capstone Press, 2017.

Summers, Alex. *Haunted Houses*. Yikes! It's Haunted. Vero Beach, FL: Rourke Educational Media, 2016.

INTERNET SITES

All about Ghosts:
https://www.cbc.ca/kidscbc2/the-feed/monsters-101-all-about-ghosts

Ghost-Hunting Tools:
http://mentalfloss.com/article/560396/ghost-hunting-tools-recommended-paranormal-investigators

One-Third of Americans Believe in Ghosts:
https://news.gallup.com/poll/17275/onethird-americans-believe-dearly-may-departed.aspx

INDEX